TOW TRUCKS

RYAN EARLEY

TABLE OF CONTENTS

A Pelican Book

Teaching Tips for Caregivers and Teachers:

Research shows that one of the best ways for students to learn a new topic is to read about it.

Before Reading

- Read the title and predict what the book will be about.
- Read the "Words to Know" and discuss the meaning of each word.
- Read the back cover to see what the book is about.

During Reading

- When a student gets to a word that is unknown, ask them to look at the rest of the sentence to find clues to help with the meaning of the unknown word.
- Motivate students with praise and encouragement.

After Reading

- Discuss the main idea of the book.
- Ask students to give one detail that they learned in the book.

Sight Words

a
all
four
have
help
is
some
this

Words to Know

flatbed

tow truck

wheels

winch

yoke

This is a **tow truck.**

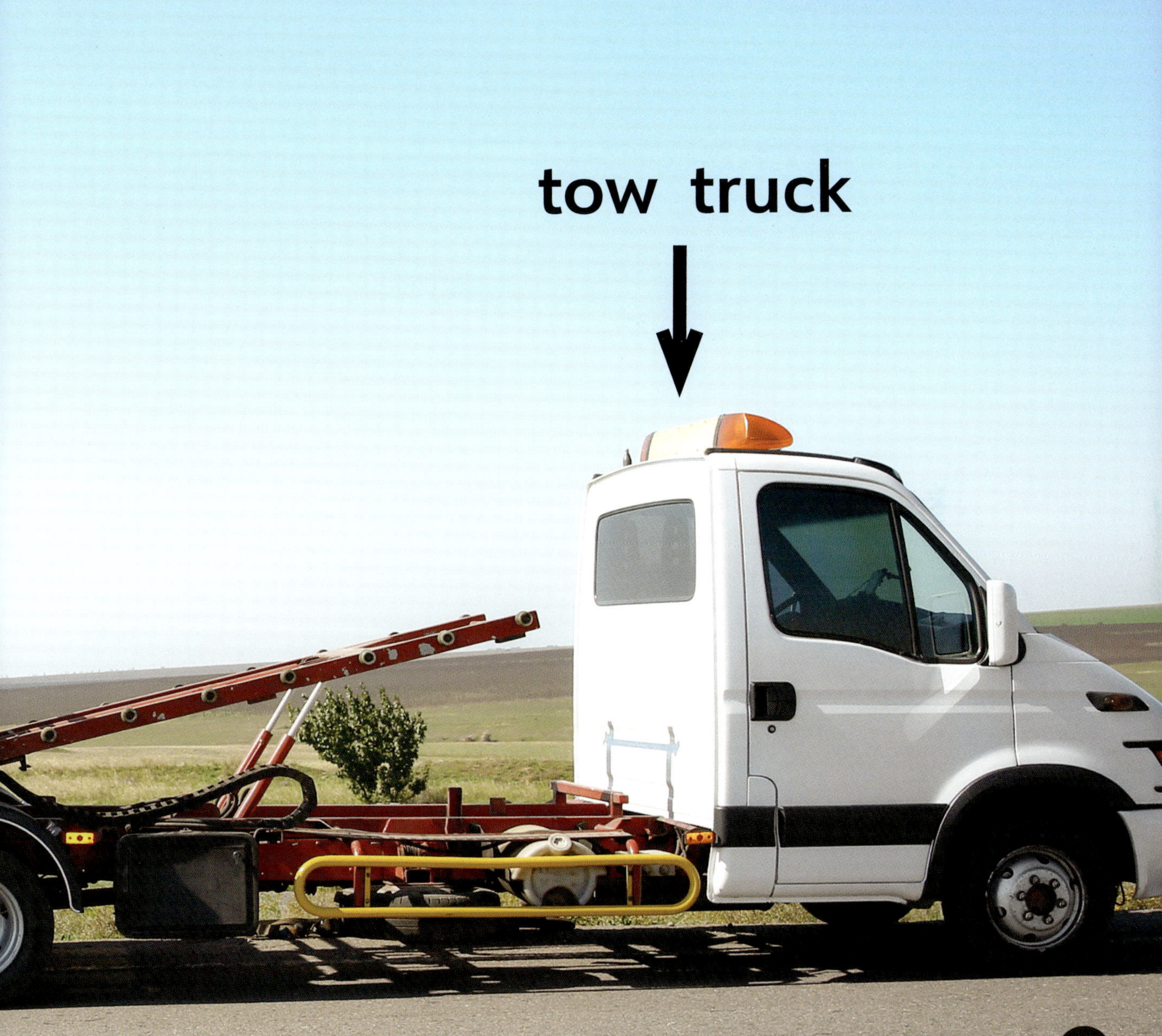
tow truck

All tow trucks have four **wheels**.

wheel

Some tow trucks have a **flatbed**.

Some tow trucks have a **winch**.

winch

Some tow trucks have a **yoke**.

-818-888
yoke

All tow trucks help!

Index

Written by: Ryan Earley
Design by: Savina Magaro
Editor: Kim Thompson
Series Development: James Earley

Photos: aappp: cover; New Africa: p. 4-5; Oatautta: p. 7; Klara_Steffkova: p. 8-9; Virrage Images: p. 11; Thamkc: p. 13; Grisha Bruert: p. 15

Library of Congress PCN Data
Tow Trucks / Ryan Earley
Mighty Trucks
ISBN 978-1-6389-7948-7(hard cover)
ISBN 979-8-8873-5007-3(paperback)
ISBN 979-8-8873-5066-0(EPUB)
ISBN 979-8-8873-5125-4(eBook)
Library of Congress Control Number: 2022942272
Printed in the United States of America.

Seahorse Publishing Company
seahorsepub.com 1-800-387-7650

Published in the United States
Seahorse Publishing
PO Box 771325
Coral Springs, FL 33077